The Frankenstein Book of Prayer

STEVE CASE

APOCRYPHILE
PRESS

Dedication

For Boris

Apocryphile Press
PO Box 255
Hannacroix, NY 12087
www.apocryphilepress.com

Please join our mailing list at www.apocryphilepress.com/free. We'll keep you up-to- date on all our new releases, and we'll also send you a FREE BOOK. Visit us today!

Contents

Acknowledgments

Special thanks to:

- Eric Case for pictures and insight.
- Bob Wells, Chuck Schodowksi, and Marty Sullivan for a wasted youth in front of the television.
- Rev. Richard McCandless who didn't care what color my *Book of Common Prayer* was.
- Trader Joes because I always acknowledge Trader Joes in hopes they might shoot me some free coffee and JoJo Cookies due the amount consumed in any of my writing projects
- Caleb Metcalf—I figure three more years and he'll be old enough to watch the movie with me.
- John Mabry for patience
- Becky for love and patience beyond my comprehension.

Introduction

In Cleveland, Ohio, in the 1970s, local TV stations only had so much network programming on any given day, and the rest of the time, they had to fill in with local programming. On Friday nights, at about 11:30, after Dick Goddard (Cleveland's most beloved weatherman) finished his forecast, WJKW would bring out two crazy guys who went by the names Hoolihan and Big Chuck. They would do stupid (often "borrowed") skits, read jokes sent in by viewers, and promote local events like County Fairs and charity softball games. They would also show horror moves.

There were many Hammer films from the '60s, a Martian invader flick, the occasional badly dubbed Godzilla movie, and the classics. Hoolihan and Big Chuck introduced me to the movie *Frankenstein* (1931). I love every frame of that film, from the warning at the beginning to the burning windmill collapsing in the final moments. Thus began a lifelong obsession.

I've seen all films. *The Bride of Frankenstein* and its overly dramatic remake with Sting and Mel Brooks's masterpiece *Young Frankenstein* (Puuuuuutn ona Reeeeeeeetz.) I've seen the play with Benedict Cumberbatch and the movie with a strangely shirtless Kenneth Branagh. The DC Comics depiction of the monster is surprisingly deep, and the Big Finish Audio play is easy to get lost in. Herman Munster will always have a place in my heart.

Karloff never spoke a word in the original film. Still, so many cartoon depictions have the creature speaking with Karloff's "Grinch voice." (*The Groovie Goolies*, 1970-72)

I have the toys, statues, masks, LPs, T-shirts, and buttons. As I said, it seems to be an obsession.

I finally got around to reading Mary Shelley's novel in high school, and

I learned the original character was far and away from the Universal Monster. Shelley's "creature" was one of pity and fear. He could read and write and reason and all he really wanted was to be left alone (well, and a wife. I mean, even Herman found love.)

Okay...hang all that on a separate hook for just a moment.

During college, I worked as a Summer Camp counselor at a church camp in Ohio. One week I had a camper who said he didn't like the Lord's prayer because he didn't like using the word "father." To him, "father" was the man who was either absent or abusive, so he chose to say Creator or Lord or some creative adjective to go along with God.

Guiding God
Seeing God
Listening God
Creating God
Present God

...but never "Father."

Flash forward several years, and I am now working for an Episcopal Church in Akron, where I began another lifelong collection...prayer books. I have them from multiple denominations and religions, old and new.

Follow me now; let's put all this together.

After re-reading Shelley's masterwork, I wondered how this intelligent but lost creature would pray? What a screwed-up understanding he would have of words like "Father" or "Creator." Would he want to pray to an "Our Father" or instead pray to some other descriptor...an "All-Father?"

Imagine having no concept of the divine; how would you meet God today? At some point, you may have gone to Church. You may even know the stories from Vacation Bible School. Maybe you didn't and bought this book solely because you are a fan of classic monster movies like me. Whether a believer, agnostic, or die-hard atheist, imagine being introduced to God as a grown adult. What would you ask of this seemingly vengeful, jealous, loving, guiding Creator?

If the creature found a satchel of books in the forest and learned to speak and reason by listening with his ear to the wall of the DeLacey family home, how would the creature pray? What would he pray for? Wouldn't he have the same prayers as the rest of us?

Who am I?
What is my purpose?
Are you listening?
Do you love me? How? Why?

These are not the prayers of the lumbering mumbling giant of the black &white movie (with due respect to Mr. Karloff). These are the prayers of a rational being of such malformation that it would hurt to look at him. He was a creature of anger and pity, of pain and intelligence.

I began to imagine this solitary being start writing down his prayers as best as he understood the concept of prayer, A manuscript of liturgies and prayers that eventually finds its way into the hands of a priest who, despite the horror, the very name Frankenstein conjures, cannot bring himself to destroy the pages. Could you?

What happens when mankind starts to play God?

They said to each other, "Come, let's make bricks and bake them thoroughly." They used brick instead of stone, and tar for mortar. Then they said, "Come, let us build ourselves a city, with a tower that reaches to the heavens, so that we may make a name for ourselves. Genesis 11:3-4 (KJV)

It becomes a theme in life and in fiction.

"Even God himself could not sink this ship." —*Employee of the White Star Cruise Line (Titanic)*

"Your scientists were so preoccupied with whether or not they could, they didn't stop to think if they should." —*Ian Malcolm (Jurassic Park)*

"Open the pod bay doors, Hal." —*Dave Bowman (2001: A Space Odyssey)*

"Now I have become the destroyer of worlds." —*Robert Oppenheimer*

It never ends well.

The closer we get to perfect artificial intelligence, the closer we get to creating our own rational thinking being who may decide to just end us. (Can you say Skynet?)

Shakespeare's Richard III is rejected by society for his appearance and refers to himself as being sent before his time into the world "scarce half made up." Victor Frankenstein uses this exact phrase to describe all humans and sets out to perfect God's work. Both Walton (the ship's captain of the novel) and Victor Frankenstein allow their ambition to cloud judgment. It is their downfall.

Ultimately Mary Shelley's "creature" just wants to be accepted. By his Creator, by God, and by the world around him. We all need acceptance. We all need love and understanding. If we don't get it from our "family," we will look for it elsewhere.

The prayers in this book are inspired by Mary Shelley's creature, but let's begin with the prayer from the classic Universal movie.

It's alive. It's alive. Oh God...it's alive.

Steve Case
North Carolina
May, 2023

Preface

by the Father Joseph McCandless of St. Mary's Chapel

To Whomever Finds This Letter;

I am Father Joseph McCandless of St Mary's Chapel in Scarborough. If you have found this box and are reading this letter, I am already dead. I am beyond help and beyond helping you. I hid the box well enough and never told anyone of its existence, so I am already gone.

In this box, you will find a leather satchel. I am emploring you; burn it. Burn it along with this letter. Do not read any of the papers enclosed. I hope you are stronger than I am. Over many years I struck a match to the satchel. I even tossed it into the fireplace more than once, yet I cannot bring myself to watch it consumed. It is a secret so dark, yet I have not been able to rid myself of it. The manuscript has haunted me. Do what I could not and burn the pages before you begin reading.

The man who gave me this box and this charge did so because he could not bear their weight, nor could he destroy them. He gave the task to me, and I failed him. He was the grandson of Captain Robert Walton, who rescued a near-dead Victor Frankenstein while on a voyage to the pole. The captain claimed Frankenstein dictated the story. It was dismissed as fiction. It should have been fiction.

The name Frankenstein sits like a curse upon the lips in certain parts of this country. You know doubt have heard the word. If you do not, it is to your benefit. Perhaps he is forgotten, but I doubt this. There were always stories of what Victor Frankenstein did, of what he created. I tell you this unequivocally. They are all true.

The abomination Victor Frankenstein created was genuine. It could read. It could think. It could comprehend the mysteries of God. I believe it knew what it was. It must have been a being of such pity it would hurt to look at it.

I believe the creature had a soul. I do not know how to explain this. It goes against all I believe and all I have been taught. I know it to be true. I have struggled with this for many years and can admit it to myself and my God. I ask God's forgiveness. I do not pretend to know his ways, but I know what I say is true. The creature had a soul.

The creature prayed. This is why I cannot destroy the box and its contents. When the creature lived in the forests, it found refuge near a family home. It listened to them. It spoke with at least one of them. It discovered their books. It learned to read and to reason.

It spoke to God. It wrote its prayers down like a schoolboy writing an assignment for catechism class. It desired mercy, love, grace, forgiveness, and all we wish from the one who created us all.

The Frankensteins are no more. They died off, and those who kept the name were driven off. Their name exists only on gravestones and papers.

Make their absence permanent. Erase them from all history. Burn this box and its contents. May God forgive me for allowing it to exist behind the walls of the rectory for so long. I could not bring myself to do the deed. For God's sake, do not publish them.

Blessings Upon You,

Fr Joseph McCandless

The Prayers of the Monster

Father?

Father's
Father's
Father's
Father's
Father's
Father's
Father's
Father...

please help me.

Father, Creator, Lord, God,
The family in the next room
speaks your names.
They talk with you.
They believe you created them.
You created everything.

You did not create me.
I was created by another father.
You are father to all.

Are you father to me?

Are you the all-father?
The family calls you the Our-Father.
I read their books.
There is one that they read
more than any other.

They say it is your book.
I watch them through the hole in the wall
and have learned to read your book.

You are an angry father.
My father is also angry.
You also show pity and mercy
and kindness and forgiveness.
My father shows none of these.

The De Laceys say you love everyone.
No one can do this. Not even you.
No father loves all his children.

All Father,

Do you make it with your hands?
The De Laceys say you made everything
with your hands.

I look at my hands.
They are not the hands of a creator.
My father was a creator,
and his hands created life like yours.

He did a bad job.
Most of your work is beautiful.
I am not beautiful.
My hands are not my own.

They are made of others hands.
I see four other men in my hands.
Sometimes I can see the life
inside their skins.

My skin.

It moves like the waters in the streams.
De Lacey uses his hands to love his family.
I want to use my hands to end mine.
I will end my Father.

All-Father,

Is there memory in the skin?
Is there memory in ones eyes?

I see the sunrise with these eyes
I know are not mine,
and its like I remember it.

These eyes have seen sunrises,
but I have not.
This tongue has tasted water
from streams, but I have not.
These ears have heard thunder.
The thunder feels so soon.

I feel like I am part of the world
in a way that the people around me are not.
I am part of the air and the water.
Yet I am disconnected from it.

I am in between.
I dont like it in between.

All-Father,

I found the books in the woods.
A leather satchel protected them
from the damp.
I knew what they were,
that they possessed stories and knowledge.

The De Laceys have many.
The woman taught her son to read.
The old man with the broken eyes helped.
The boy learned to read
and to speak by reading and by sound.

I sat behind the wall, and I listened too.
If I sat quietly, they lived their lives,
and I learned so much.
I think one of those inside me
was a learned man, but I dont know.

Learning is not difficult for me,
but there is no one I can speak to about it.

There was no one to give me praise as the
mother praised her boy for his lessons.
The boy had his books, and I had mine.

I took mine into the caves,
and I spoke the words aloud.
I could hear my words repeat themselves
in the cave. I could listen to the words.

Then I found your book.

The old man said it was a book
above all others.
There are stories and poems, and rules.

It was a book of life.
Life should be shared, should it not?

All-Father,

What is the family?

Sometimes I put my hands
on the dwelling of the De Laceys.
I feel its warmth as I peer through
a hole in the wall.
Sometimes I can feel the blood running in
the veins of my hands
that are not my hands.

I can feel life in the walls of this house.
They sing.
The old man likes it when they sing.

I think the old man can feel
the vibration in the walls too.
They sing. They tell stories.
Sometimes they read to the old man
from your book.
Sometimes the old man tells stories
from the book.

The old mans eyes don't work.
Mine do.

I would give him my eyes,
but I don't know how.
If my father could make my eyes see,
could he do that for the old man?
If the healer in your book could make
the blind see.
Can you?

Why don't you?

All Father,

Today I put on the long robe
and walked to the river.
I understand there are more rivers.
There are rivers and streams,
and they lead to bigger things.

I held my hand up to the sun
and saw the blood running in my skin.
I am like a river.
I am the wood and the fields and the city.
Rivers run through me.

The woman, the sister-daughter,
she is sad much of the time.
She worries for the old man.
I suspect she will worry about someone else
when he dies.

What happens to the dead?
What was supposed to happen to me?
The old man tells the boy

that death is like sleeping.
Was I asleep?
Am I what happens when the dead wake up?
I do not want the old man
to become like me.
I do not need walls to feel separated.

The old man smiles when
he believes they are watching him.
The sister-daughter.
She watches the old man.
She is worried for him.

Her sadness affects everything.

All-Father,

You fashioned Your Adam from the clay.
Did You take Your time?
There is fine pottery
and pottery that was thrown quickly.
A bowl is not a bowl if it is not centered.
A cup with too much clay at the lip
is hard to drink from.
So, did You take Your time?

Was Your Adam beautiful?
As compared to what?
There were no other Adams.
No people to compare him to.

Did You think he was good
along with the rest of Your creations?
Earth-Father did not take his time.

He worried so much if all parts would work,
he didn't take time to wonder
what would happen if they did.

He didn't plan for success.

The first face I can remember seeing
was one of revulsion.
My father looked at mine
and ran screaming from the room.

Did you turn your back on your own creation?
I look at them. I wear the cloak,
and I sit in the shadows.
Some men bathe in rosewater,
and others sit in the puddles.

Where is fairness?
Where is the respect for your creation?
Are they not all breathing the same air?
Are they not all descended
from your Adam? Your Eve?

Am I a monster purely because of my face?
Earth-father did not concern himself
with such things.
An eye socket from here.

An ear from there.
Teeth, tongue, nose
Stich, stitch stitch.

The smooth skin of a young man
across my chest.
Something wrinkled and elderly on my leg.

I am no man.
I am a flesh-quilt.
Your Jesus, could he heal me, make me whole?
Would he? Or am I dammed?

I was dammed before any of this began.
I was dammed before my first scream.

Amen.

All-Father,

Today the boy asked his grandfather
about the word Amen.
They say it when they speak to You.
The boy wanted to know what it meant.

So do I.

The old man says it means, "Let it be so."
The boy asked why they said it two times.
The old man says the second time means, "Make
it so."

I will say this word to You.
Amen & Amen.

All-Father,

Am I an angel?
Is that what I am?
Your book says people hide if fright
when an angel comes near.

I began taking food
and firewood from the family.
Then I saw they were as hungry as I was.
I stopped.

I lived off what I found in the forest
and began to leave food and wood
on the familys doorstep at night.

I heard them. They said it must have been
an angel You sent to protect them.
To save them from starvation.
Am I an angel?

Why am I afraid to let them see me?
Amen and Amen.

All-Father,

It is only my face that enrages people.
I sat with the old man today.
We spoke of life and of nature.

We spoke of the birds he liked to listen to.
We spoke of music,
and he played his instrument for me.

He is the only other human who has not
run from my face.
Why do people assume evil about me?

I was not created as other men.
I was fashioned together. I understand that.
Sometimes it is almost like
I can hear their voices.

The voices inside me.
The voices that make me who I am.

Sometimes they weep.

Sometimes they grow angry.

I think the eyes in my head
were the eyes of a learned man.
I can read.
I can comprehend.

I found the books in the shed
behind the house, and I listened to
the family read.
It was not difficult.

I want to ask my father who I was.
What other men do I come from?

The old man has no eyes, yet he can see me.
In my voice, he can see the man I am.
Why is the man with no eyes
the only one who can see me?

Amen & Amen.

All-Father,

My hands are nearly perfect.
There is a scar on my wrist
below the hastily sewn one.
It is from the previous owner.
The way my hands fit together,
interlacing fingers.
The way they sound when I clap.
They are from the same person.

Who did Earth-Father take them from?
Was he a musician?
A surgeon? A doctor like my father?
Would they remember the music they made?
They are not the hands of a laborer.

I write these words to you in this book,
and I don't remember learning how
to hold a pen.

No one taught me.

Instinct or memory.

I am sorry to those whose parts
are now part of me.
I am sorry for what you have become.
This should not be the end of your story.

I will go away when I end my earth-father's
story, and you all can rest.

All-father make them whole in your house.
They should not be blamed for what I am,

For what my earth-father made.

All Father,

I walked among them today.
Your other children.
The beautiful ones.
Their hair is long and thick.
Their skin has no scars.

The old man gave me a cloak with a hood,
and I hid my face.
So many walk with their heads bowed down
that they don't notice me.

I tower over them.
I could break any of them.

I saw an old woman with a cloak
made of other cloaks.
The stitches were crude and coarse.
Her cloak looks like my face and arms.

The old man has told his son
of the friend who comes to see him.
I have heard them talking.

The woman is frightened
that the old man is unwell in his mind.

The old man keeps repeating verses
from your book about welcoming strangers.
I believe the old man knows where
the food and firewood come from.

Thank you all-father for my friend.
I do not believe we are meant to be alone.
The old man says you are a friend to all,
but as I only speak to you
and cannot hear your voice
or feel the hand of friendship on my shoulder,
I will take his word for it.

I will meet the old mans family.

Amen & Amen.

All-Father

Make them all blind.

Amen & Amen.

All-Father,

The family will probably starve.
I suspect the woman will die first;
she is the weakest.

She is also the kindest.

She goes without food
so the others can eat.

Her husband is strong but not very smart.
The old man is as tough as stone but sick.

I met them.

I sat with the old man.
I took the cloak he gave me from my face,
and we sat by the warm fire.

He said, They are coming.

He seemed happy for them to meet me

as if he could finally prove to the woman
he was not out of his mind.

The husband came after me with his ax.
Make them all blind, All-Father.
Then they can see.

Amen and Amen.

All-Father,

Who gets to be called Saint?

I have read in the books I took
from the family about Your Saint Christopher.
The family went away and left
many things behind, including books.
I stayed in their cabin.
I was warmed by their fire.
Then I heard angry voices
coming in the night.

I took my cloak. I took some books.
I have been reading about
Your servants they call saints.

Beside the river, I saw a boy.
He would have drowned.
I think he called for You,
but the water filled his cries.
I pulled him out.

He clung to me so hard.
He was not afraid of me.

His father shot at me.

I sat by this fire tonight
and pulled the bullet from my shoulder
with my knife.

I read about your Saint Christopher,
who carried children across the river.

Was he as strong as I am?
Did they accuse him?
Fear him? Attack him?
Why do I have no place?

Amen and Amen.

All Father,

You made life in Your hands,
and You make death in Your hands.
The power of life and death.
You choose.

I know what this is now.
I know what You feel.
I found my father's brother.

He was a child.
He did not fear me.
He did not run from my face.

He looked at me, and I saw my father.
They had the same eyes.
The boy was curious.
He stared at me in wonder.
I could see his amazement.
He did not see a monster.
He should have.
Amen & Amen.

All-Father,

They have accused a woman
of murdering my fathers brother.
Was he my brother too?

I was not made. I was created.
Do I have brothers? Sisters?

The woman who has been accused
is the woman charged with his care.
She screams she is innocent.

At night I put my hands
on the building where she is kept.
She cries all night.

Blind-her.
She should not see what is coming.

Amen and Amen.

All-Father,

I saw my creator, my father.
He is here.
He saw me, and he knew.

He knew I was the one who took
young William from this world.

What did my father do?

He said nothing.
He knows she is innocent,
Yet he is so ashamed of me
that he would let her die
rather than acknowledge me.

They call me a monster.

Amen and Amen.

All-Father,

I watched my father's face
when the woman was hanged.
He did not see me.
His face was a stone,
but I could see his soul.

He let her die.
He could have stopped it.

What emotion is that?
I have seen many,
but I do not know that one.

The DeLacys say that the woman
will be taken to You.
The innocent belong to You.
The boy is with You, is he not?
He was not responsible for his name.
I saw in his face he would become his name.
No one should become a Frankenstein.
No one.

All-Father,

I am not a man.
I am men.
There are others inside me.
Sewn into me.

Sometimes I hear them.
Sometimes I feel their thoughts.
They are confused. They are angry.
They are afraid.

I ignore them.

There is no original me.
There is a real me.
I wonder if Earth-father understood that.
Did he think that maybe those he used
would remember being alive?

I do not think so, All-Father.
I think he allowed his desire
to be you to confuse him.

Blind him.

I am the one with someone elses eyes,

and he is the one who is blind.

I will make him see what he did.

I will make him hear their screams.

Then he will know.

He must be taught to understand.

I will make him know death is not permanent.

Amen.

All-Father,

I do not understand what emotion this is.
I have been so cold lately.
I have slept in a cave
with a blanket I stole from a house.

I have been so cold.

Today there is sun.
Today there is warmth.
I have heard a villager say
it is called Spring.
I have read this word,
but I do not understand it.
Does it mean life?
Are we given Spring?

My mind and skin react
to the memories of those
whose pieces are now mine.
They remember.

They feel this spring.
It is painful for them
because of where they are.

Did You grant them death All-Father?
Did You accept them?
Are these just leftover memories, I feel?

What I feel is so close to being new.
Is it hope?
Have You allowed me to feel hope?

Amen & Amen.

All-Father,

Are we meant to know what You know?
This Spring,
This return of the sun
and the green in the trees
This hope

Are we meant to know where it comes from?
The seed brings the flower.
The egg brings the hawk.
Are we meant to know where it began?

My heart beats.
I can put my hand on my own chest
and feel it.

I can breathe in and feel the air inside me.
I can taste the water from the stream
and feel it cool me all the way down.

Is there a spring in me?
Do I have a soul?

The old man said all men have souls.
I am no man.
You give souls when we are born.
I was not born.
I don't think I am meant to be alive,
but I am.

I don't know if I have a soul,
but I feel something in me awakens.
I see Your dawn every day.
I see Your moon and Your stars.
If we keep asking why or where
do we stop seeing the spring?
Can we know too much?

My earth-father pushed the limits.
He created me.
He did not know what he was doing?
He did not know about the soul?
Perhaps no one can make a soul but You,
All-Father.

All-Father,

I walk among them.
I wear a cloak and lean on a cane,
and people walk around me.

I'm seen and unseen.
Men see me and walk with their arm
around their woman. Protecting her.

I am unlike any other man.
I need a woman unlike any other woman.
I need a woman like me.
Made from the parts of other women.
Made by the hands of my father.

I must find Frankenstein and make him
build me a mate.
She and I can go.
Go away. Far away.
Somewhere we can be alone.

You fashioned an Eve for Adam.

Was she not made of parts?
I will find my father
and make him make me an Eve.

Amen and Amen.

All-Father,

Send life.
You send life to a mother
with her child in the womb.
You sent life in the storm that created me.
Brought me back from a death
I have no memory of.

You sent life in the beginning.
Your book says the world was void.
There was only darkness.
Is this darkness where I came from?
I did not appear as ordinary men do.
I came from darkness.
There was light,
and then I became
became
Am I your creation, or am I his?
Am I my own?
If I ask him to make me an Eve
am I asking for someone else
to live my life of struggle?

Of pain?

Of emptiness?

Or am I asking for someone to share mine?

He will not want to help me.

I will make him.

Amen & Amen.

All-Father,

I found him, All-Father.
I found my earth-father.
Why did I fear him?
He is a small man.
His power was in his mind.
I could see it in his eyes.
Now he is tired and weak.

He knows what I did.
He feels the responsibility of his creation.
Do you feel this?
Do you look down from your castle
and see what your creation does?
When Cain killed Able did you feel loss?
Guilt? Pain?

Your creations have been killing
each other for a long time.
Sometimes to impress you.
Sometimes despite you.

My earth-father looks at me
with hatred and remorse.
He regrets me.

Do you regret your children?
I pity him.

Amen & Amen.

All-Father,

Do I have the right to be happy?

I have air inside me.
My eyes see. My tongue speaks.
Do I have the right to what
any other being has?
Do I have the right to love?

Do I have the right to a companion
to share my struggle and to share hers?

My earth-father hates me.
He wants me to be gone
so he can live his own life,
but he can't as long as I live.

If he makes me an Eve,
I will take her, and we will leave.
We will go someplace else
and be alone...She and I.
He can have his life.

He can have his bride.
He can put his guilt
on a high shelf and never touch it.

All-Father,

What is my name?
You have so many, but when someone
in your book asks, you are evasive.
How do people call on you?
Perhaps they don't need to.
Perhaps you can't be called
if you are never away.

I have no name.
Like you, I have no name.
My earth father called me abomination,
but that is not a name.
I will take my earth-father's name.
I am Frankenstein.

It is not just who I am; it is what I am.
I am no man. I am no monster.
I am no angel or saint.
I am no abomination.
I am Frankenstein.

Amen and Amen.

All Father,

Your book says you formed
your Adam from the clay.
You had to come down here
and form the being with your own hands.
Like a potter.
Like a child playing with dough.

You made your Adam and then
breathed life into him.
Adam was never a child, yet he was a man.
I am a man who was never a child.
I watch my earth-father
at work in his laboratory.

I watch him create a woman with his hands.
She is like me.
She will go away with me,
and we will be alone.

I will leave the earth-father to his life,
and he will leave me to mine.
Me and my Eve. Amen and Amen.

All-Father,

He killed her.
Before she had breath.
Before her eyes could see.
Before I could hear her voice.
Before I could touch her hand.
He killed her.

He tore apart his own creation.
He is no God.
He is no giver of life.
He is evil.

His laboratory is ash.
I burned it, but he ran away.
I will find him. I will end his life.
Not his breath. Not his mind.
I will end all he loves.
I will take away his friends.
I will take away the light of his eyes.
His Eve.
His Elizabeth.

I will feel her warm neck.
I will see the fear in her eyes.
I will let her understand what I am.

I am Frankenstein.
She will know what I am, whose I am
When I end her.
I will make my earth-father know loss.

Amen & Amen.

All-Father,

The man Henry was so easy to kill.
The boy, the young Frankenstein,
at least he struggled.

When he finally understood
what was happening, he fought
At least he tried.

He will be the last Frankenstein.
There will be no more.
My earth-father is a Frankenstein,
but he committed himself to his own death
when he broke apart my Eve.

He is already dead.
He just does not know it.
Death follows him.
Henry didn't believe
what was happening to him.
Perhaps his mind broke first,
and he didn't allow himself to believe.

He somehow was able to suspend belief.
Even as my hand closed
over his mouth and nose.
He didn't struggle.

He died believing he couldnt possibly be dying.
Monsters cant possibly be real.
The boy believed.
The boy already knew monsters exist.

Amen and Amen.

All-Father,

Forgive me.
Forgive my actions.
Your book says to honor
my father and mother.
I have no mother.

The people who think they can be you
get into the most trouble.
The people who built the tower
to be higher than you
were scattered to the winds.

Kings and Queens who thought themselves
God were silenced.
My earth-father thought he could create life.
He thought he could be you.
The weight of it was too much
for his tiny mind.

I am merely your servant.
I will end the pretender.

Amen & Amen.

All-Father,

She had never seen anything ugly.
Her entire life was spent
away from painful things.
Unpretty things.

I'm sure she always had flowers.
She always had lace.
She always had colors.

When she was cold,
someone brought her a blanket
When she was hungry,
someone brought her food.
I'm sure there was a flower on the tray.

Her life was spent without ever knowing
that anything ugly existed.
She had no concept of anything
that didn't smell nice or look pretty.

I was such a shock to her.

Some deep part of her mind
tried to tell her it was a nightmare,
but what is a nightmare
to someone who has never seen
anything not pretty?

She could not grasp my existence.
She didnt know how to scream in fear.
She didnt know how to scream.
I didnt even have to try.

Young William struggled.
Henry just let it happen to him.
But Father's Eve, his Elizabeth.
She died knowing fear for the first time.
I didnt kill her.
I think she died from fright.

Amen and Amen.

All-Father,

I am alone.
Are You?
You have no equal.
There is just You.

My earth-father believed he was alone,
but he made that himself.
He thought he was better
than everyone else.
He felt he had to lower himself
to spend time with others.
He thought that was part of being God.

All things have an opposite.
Dark. Light. Up. Down.
Left. Right. Beginning. End.
You and You alone are singular.

I should not exist.
I wanted earth-father to make me
a companion, so I was not singular.

He did not do it for me.
He did it so I would leave him alone.

Then he was afraid we would become more.

I.

We.

More.

How do you accept your aloneness,
your singularity?
You created a universe.
You created your own family,
and so many of them denied you exist.
They say you are not possible.
They say I am not possible.
Yet here we are.

You desire companionship so much
you create life.
I desire to be alone so much
I am willing to end it.

Amen & Amen.

All-Father,

Take them in.
Elizabeth
William
Henry
The old man DeLacey,
I'm sure he is dead by now.

Take them in like lost children.
They died because of my earth-Father.
He should have stayed
with his books and his lessons.
He did not, and now he is alone too.
He should be.

Amen and Amen.

All-Father,

I am chased.
I have run before,
but I don't remember being chased.
Yet, I am in the woods,
in the cave, in the thicket.

Someone who is a part of me
must have been chased before.
His instinct is my instinct.
How else would I know how to run?

This is not like hiding behind the wall
in the De Lacey's home.
They did not know I was there.

I am hiding from men.
with torches and pitchforks.
They want me dead.
They don't know who I am.
My earth father chases me too.
He is full of guilt and regrets.

He is motivated by his guilt.
He chases me because he hates me.
He hates himself.

He will be chasing me long after
the others have given up.
He will chase me to the ends of the earth.
That is where I will lead him.

Let him find me there, All-Father.
Keep me safe from the
pitchforks and torches.
Let my earth-father find me.

Amen & Amen.

All-Father,

The captain of the sea vessel
did not even argue.
He did not see my face.
He did not try to.

I suspect he has given passage
to others without question.
He accepted the money I took from Henry.
I still have the silver coins
and the gold jewelry from Elizabeth.

The robe covers my face and limbs.
The sailors leave me alone
for fear of catching my disease.
My only disease is the desire to be human.
I am humans.
No one sees them but my earth-father.

Amen & Amen.

All-Father,

I did not have a childhood.
I was never a baby.
Yet, the feeling of this ship rocking,
the sound of the ship creaking,
is that what a cradle is like for an infant?
Do babies fall asleep to this sound?

At night I wandered the decks of the ship.
The watchman sees me, but he says nothing.
The crew fear me.
There was a storm a few days ago,
and the crew decided
it was somehow my fault.
They are a superstitious and cowardly lot.

They voted to see whether or not
I would make it to our destination.
The captain shut it down.
He was a man of honor,
paid to do a job,
and he would finish it.

I quoted to him from your book.
Psalm 107, "They that go down to the sea
in ships, that do business in great waters;
These see the works of the Lord
and his wonders in the deep.
For he commandeth,
and raiseth the stormy wind,
which lifteth up the waves thereof.
They mount up to the heaven,
they go down again to the depths:
their soul is melted because of trouble."

The captain thinks I am a monk or priest.
He says he will protect me from his crew.
He is an honorable man.
You do have honorable men.

Amen & Amen.

All-Father,

I do not feel the cold.
On the deck out in the stars,
I feel the wind but not the cold.

I have seen the men,
stout and strong, shiver.
They are afraid.
Afraid of death.
Afraid of loss.
Afraid of being lost.
Afraid of never returning home.
Afraid of pain.
I have experienced all of these.

I have experienced all of these
like a well that has no bottom.
I am still here.
I do not fear any of them.
Then men grow wary of my presence.

I used to listen to the conversations of the
De Laceys through the wall.
I listen to the men.
They are growing more afraid
and will soon turn on their captain
if they dont turn on each other.

I will have to leave soon.
Guide this ship, All-Father.
Send it home.

Amen & Amen.

All-Father,

My earth-father has found me.
His Eve is dead.
His brother is dead.
His friend is dead.
He seeks revenge.

I imagine he thinks
of what his life would have been
if he had listened.
If he had drowned his ambitions to be God.

He comes for me,
but it is himself that he hates.
He knows he will not come home.

He gave me life
and now is obligated to take it back.
I don't know that I can be killed.
I was not meant to be alive.
I did not ask for it.
Is my life precious to you?

Amen & Amen.

All-Father,

He is behind me.
I have not slept or needed to for days.
He will drive himself to exhaustion.
He could die out on the ice.
I am stopped and waiting for him.

I will talk with the earth-father,
the Frankenstein.
I want to hear his confession.
I will forgive him for giving me life.
No child should hate his father
the way I do mine.
How do you put up with the anger
of your children?

Protect him, All-Father.
Keep him safe.
He needs to finish his creation.
Do not take this from him.

Amen & Amen.

All-Father,

He was so close.
He could see my face and I his.
He did not turn away with revulsion.
We are beyond that.
His face was gaunt and haggard.
His grief was audible.
He has had many days
to think of what he would say.

Then the ice broke.

We were close enough to hear each other,
and the ice broke,
sounding like a tree falling.
He was pitched upward
and landed on his back
as the ice beneath his feet
rolled away from me.

He was inconsolable.
His cries were anguish.

Did he cry like that for his brother?
For his Eve?
I stood there and watched him drift away.
He surely broke his hands,
pounding the ice in his frustration.

He made me with those hands.
He is undoubtedly a dead man on the ice.
Judge him fairly, All-Father.
He has many questions.

Amen & Amen.

All-Father,

Did you bring him home?
Did he pound on your palace door
and demand answers?
Did he see the error of his ways?
Did he beg your forgiveness?
Did you grant it, or did you punish him?

Is it even possible for me to die, All-Father?
I did not come into the world
like anyone else.
I doubt I will be able to leave it
like anyone else.
Will I be able to leave it?

Is this my punishment, just staying?
Grant us all peace, All-Father.
You must be as tired as the rest of us.

Amen & Amen.

All-Father,

He lives.
The earth-father lives.
I saw the ship days ago.
Now they have stopped dead
in the ice and have found him.
They rescued him.

At night I walk from my camp
to the ship on the ice.
I listen at the walls.
I put my hands on the wood
and feel the life within.
My earth-father lives.

Amen & Amen.

All-Father,

I stood on the ice and placed my hands
on the side of the boat.
My earth-father lies within.

I feel the sun on my back,
and I know the ice is not here for long.

I hear the sailors use the word ambition.
Ambition.
I hear this word sometimes.
I heard it from the shadows
at my earth-fathers wedding.
Ambition and Obsession.
The captain of this ship
lies somewhere between.
He will put himself in danger.
He has put the lives of his crew in danger.

I dont believe this is entirely about ego.
My earth-father wanted to create life
so he could be like You.

The captain of his vessel
wants to know what is next.

The passage through the Northwest
has not been done before,
but it is what's next.
Someday men will make ships
that sail around the world.
Sometime men will touch the stars.

Because they are next.

This is ambition.
Some men will die trying
to achieve whats next.

This is obsession.

Ambition makes room
for the end goals to happen.

Obsession will risk everything
with no plan at all.

Did You make them for this?
Did You make them
constantly strive for more?
Your book says You gave mankind
everything, and they were not content.
If You made them, You must have known
this would happen.

Earth-Father had no plan.
He was obsessed.
Everything that happened afterward
is his fault.

He should have seen this coming.

Amen and Amen.

All-Father,

All my desire for revenge
All of my hatred
All of my obsessions
Are gone.

They have been drowned in a well of pity.
I kneeled by his bed.
I held his hand.
He knew I was there.
His hand closed over mine.

Did he see his child?
Did he see his Eves murderer?
Did he see a destroyer of families?
Did he see a mirror?

Did he know that I cannot join him in death?
Did he make me
to wander the earth forever?

He slipped away into death
like his ice slipped away from me days ago.
He did not scream this time.

He slid into death.
He opened his arms and welcomed it.
He is truly with you this time,
but I dont know
that he will ever know peace.
And I will never be able to ask him.

The captain of the ship saw me.
He is a brave man with
the want of knowledge in his hands,
but I saw no ego.

I did not see a man who would question you,
only a man with questions.
I wonder what stories he told.

Amen & Amen.

All-Father,

I am to take these pages
and put them with the books
I stole from the De Laceys home.

I have carried them with me for so long.
I will put them on the sled,
and I will send the dogs on their way
and let Providence decide on their existence.

I am determined to sleep.
If I cannot die, then I can at least stop.
Like the waters frozen in place,
they can at least stop.

The further north I go,
the less the ice flows.
There must be a place
where everything can just stop.

The blood that is not mine
can cease flowing in the limbs

that are not mine.
We can all just stop.
Can't we, Father?

Amen & Amen.